TO ENCOURAGE THE OTHERS

The Court Martial and Example of Admiral John Byng

A Play

by

Nigel Pascoe

*Cover image from **The National Maritime Museum, Greenwich, UK**. Artist unknown.*

ISBN: 978-1-326-45306-0

PublishNation, London
www.publishnation.co.uk

Preface

The Court Martial of Admiral Byng in 1757 remains a controversial and unsatisfactory trial. Further, in the light of the findings of the Court, the necessary imposition of the mandatory sentence was plainly unjust. As Byng himself argued, if negligence was a proper basis for conviction, that should have meant gross negligence and not merely errors of judgement. Any other construction,

"might expose the bravest man that ever commanded to the severest penalties, since a single error in judgment might render him liable to the most capital punishment."

Byng did not deserve to lose his life, but the harsh Articles of War then existing allowed no lesser penalty. He was an example and died courageously. This play is dedicated to his memory and the fervent hope of his descendants that, one day, Right will prevail.

I have set the scene as a 21st century lecture at the Britannia Royal Naval College, Dartmouth. That permits contemporary comparisons, for those so inclined.

The play is adaptable for a number of voices. The Fourth Voice should be female. I have included specific scenes, although, except for a short interval, it should run continuously. Amongst other places, it has been performed at Greenwich before HRH The Princess Royal and in the Temple Church, London.

I would like to express my thanks to the many people who have helped me to research and present this play at different times and inspired me by their commitment. They include my wife Elizabeth, Thayne Byng, Sarah Saunders-Davies, Dr J David Davies, Carolyn Martin, Gill Richards, Ken Madine, Sir Michael Morland, David Hobart, Brian Harris QC, Dom Young, Commodore Timothy Harris RN, Lieutenant Gareth Mawdsley RN, all cast members, Dimity Pascoe for the sound recording and all my children. My apologies to anyone that I have omitted. All should be assured that the responsibility for the final text is mine alone, notwithstanding the excellent advice which I have received!

March 2007
Revised September 2015   **Nigel Pascoe**

A Note to the Players...

I have been extremely fortunate in having had some very talented players in the different productions of this play. Byng has been played by Richard Tutt, Richard Ritchie, Chris Ware and Anthony Arlidge. Elizabeth Pascoe, my wife, has played the Fourth Voice throughout and other outstanding readers have included Frank Abbott, George Dibben, Peter Cowell, Christopher Parker and Mathew Scott. To all members of all casts, I want to extend my heartfelt thanks for their skill and support. No author could have been better served.

SCENES

1. Britannia Royal Naval College, Dartmouth - a naval lecture

2. Byng introduced – Historical setting – Summary of Engagement on May 20th 1756

3A. Court Martial – The Evidence

Interval

SCENE 1

Britannia Royal Naval College, Dartmouth

Music - Cue 1: The Band of Her Majesty's Royal Marines

FIRST VOICE *(standing)*

Our distinguished guest lecturer this evening needs no introduction from me. So I simply want to say, as Commodore, that we are delighted and privileged that the Second Sea Lord has chosen to come back here to the Britannia Royal Naval College for this, his last engagement before he retires. Please give him a very warm welcome. *(Leads cast clapping)*

Second Sea Lord stands at lectern

SECOND SEA LORD

Thank you for your kind invitation. Forty years ago as a young naval cadet, I sat where you are sitting - and I have not forgotten what an uncomfortable experience that was! There have, of course, been many changes. No women cadets in my time graced the building: at least, not officially!

No - I have nothing but affectionate memories of this place – first as a cadet and then a few years back, also as Commodore for a spell. No doubt that is tempered by the amnesia of senior moments!

But if tonight you detect a hint of nostalgia, then you will remember that today, I retire. This morning, I left the Ministry of Defence buoyed up by the best champagne the civil service has to offer. Well not vintage perhaps, but I am pleased to report that naval tradition continued on my arrival and that later this evening we can all look forward to an excellent dinner – and the legendary capacity of your Commodore yet again can be put to the test!

All of which means that tonight - I can say precisely what I like. It is, I confess, an exhilarating feeling.

(Pause)

But it is also a sobering one. For here I learned my trade in arms. Here I made friendships that have lasted a lifetime. Some sadly ending in the business that is our duty. The service of our country in time of war.

I am tempted to say that since I joined Dartmouth, I have enjoyed every minute of my Service. Very easy to say.

(Pause)

But that would be wrong. And tonight is no time for rosy illusions. Let me tell you why.

For the last five years of my service until 1200 hours this afternoon, I have spent my working hours in the company of civil servants and senior politicians. A Whitehall Warrior, no less. It is an uneasy and sometimes slippery relationship. The politician and the serviceman. Those who talk and we who must act. For ultimately they may send us to fight the wars that they have chosen.

It has been an interesting experience - but one that frankly I would not wish on my worst enemy. Imagine running the daily risk of being marginalised by the mandarins of Whitehall – all those very clever Oxbridge double Firsts, and each one so charming. Let me tell you plainly - it can be very frustrating. But that, ladies and gentlemen, in a nutshell, is what happened to me. So I decided finally that it was no place for a simple sailor.

But nor am I the first Admiral or senior serviceman to suffer under this particular yoke. By no means. So tonight, given by the present Commodore a completely free hand in my choice of subject – and here in the institution that launched me – certain of your absolute discretion, I want to end my career with a few home truths and a very salutary story.

A tale of another sailor who fell out with the powers that be. Stigmatised by press and public alike. As he put it himself,

BYNG *(seated)*

'It is my misfortune to have laboured under the disadvantage of a popular and almost national prejudice.'

2SL

An officer whose actions I invite you to judge again. Remember please only this - not for a moment is this a story of cowardice. It begins in the Autumn - of 1755.

MUSIC – Cue 2

Lights on to period map of Europe
Second Sea Lord takes up long pointer

2SL

Minorca. The Falklands of its day. Taken by us from Spain, together with Gibraltar, in the War of the Spanish Succession. In Port Mahon, a dockyard, vital to our naval operations in the Mediterranean. The colony now an obvious target for the French. And very poorly defended that October. For His Majesty's Government - led by the 1ˢᵗ Duke of Newcastle had failed miserably to protect it.

The officer in command of the island was General William Blakeney. Aged eighty two. Early retirement was not yet in fashion!

THIRD VOICE/ General Blakeney *(seated – an old Voice)*

And just as well, as it turned out…

2SL

The garrison was particularly weak and worse than that, most of the officers were on leave. Not therefore a very promising situation should the French decide to invade. And in October that year, that is exactly what our present European partners had in mind.

Indeed the British Ministry had intelligence of an expedition being prepared at Toulon in Southern France for that very purpose. *Good* intelligence, you understand! Our total naval forces in the area were three ships of the line and a few small boats. So putting it bluntly, things were not looking too good.

Well, by the beginning of 1756, the general public got wind of the danger. Something must be done.

FOURTH VOICE *(seated)*

March 11th 1756. My brother, Vice Admiral the Honourable John Byng - appointed to the command of a fleet, with orders to proceed forthwith to Minorca.

2SL

Interesting man, Byng. Time that we learnt something about him...

SCENE 2

BYNG *(stand)*

I knew these waters well. In the War of the Austrian succession, I had held senior command there. And of course, it was in the family tradition.

Our father had been a great naval hero: George Byng - or the first Viscount Torrington, as he became. Admiral of the Fleet and destroyer of the Spaniard fleet: Cape Passaro, 1718.

So naturally I wanted this command! I had the connections. I sought it. And I won it. *(Sit)*

2SL

Unfortunately the First Sea Lord, Lord Anson, did not approve of this appointment. He thought John Byng, fifty two at the time, lacked initiative, leadership and popularity. Above all, he thought him over-cautious. And Lord Anson detested that.

FIRST VOICE: LORD ANSON

I don't know how it comes to pass that, unless our Commanders in Chief have a very great superiority of the enemy, they never think themselves safe.

2SL

But central to this story was the weakness of our forces on land and at sea. Lord Anson saw the threat to Minorca as very small beer. The real threat from the French must lie in the English Channel.

The Invasion scare. Particularly of the collective consciousness of a maritime nation. And then - a very present fear.

So Byng had at his command initially only ten ships. The fleet equipped and manned with difficulty and with neither hospital nor fire ship. Their overall condition was poor. His second in command was Rear Admiral West, a popular and courageous officer, who was universally respected.

On board the little fleet were –

FIRST VOICE

A regiment of Royal Fusiliers under Lord Robert Bertie, to be landed at Gibaltar:

SECOND VOICE

Major General Stuart Lord Effingham and Colonel Cornwallis, whose regiments were in garrison at Minorca

2SL

About forty inferior officers and nearly a hundred recruits - as a reinforcement to St Philip's fortress on the island. So not much of an invasion force by any standards. Willingly or otherwise, John Byng had drawn the short straw. It was to cost him his life.

In April 1756, before he set sail, Admiral Byng certainly made his views known.

BYNG *(Seated)*

My Lords, these ships will be no match for the enemy!

2SL

But Lord Anson took a different view.

FIRST VOICE: LORD ANSON

I declare, Sir, that Byng's squadron can beat anything the French have.

2SL

And that before he had sought to engage with the enemy. If that is what he did. We need now to understand a key part of Byng's instructions.

THIRD VOICE

If, upon your arrival at Gibraltar, you shall not gain intelligence of a French squadron having passed the Straits, you are to go on, without a moment's loss of time, to Minorca.

And if you find any attack made upon that island by the French, you are to use all possible means in your power for its relief.

If you find no such attack made, you are to proceed off Toulon and station your squadron in the best manner you shall be able for preventing any French ships getting out of that port - or for intercepting and seizing any that may get out.

And you are to exert the utmost vigilance therein and in protecting Minorca and Gibraltar from any hostile attempt.

FOURTH VOICE

May 2nd 1756. Vice Admiral's fleet reaches Gibraltar.

2SL

A good starting point when we consider his later Court Martial.

Byng wrote from Gibraltar to the Lords of the Admiralty. He was angry again - with good reason - about the state of the magazine, the supplies and the lack of preparations. The place was a shambles.

BYNG

Even if it be possible, it would be very unwise to throw any men into St Philip's Castle at Minorca - as it will only add to the number that will fall into the hands of the enemy.

2SL

Dangerous stuff to send to their Lordships, but Byng was entirely right. In hindsight, it cannot have made him popular. So the stage was set for a naval and military disaster.

For when Byng set sail for Minorca on May 8th – with only two hundred or so soldiers - the French had already landed an Army of fifteen thousand troops on the Island and sufficient artillery to overwhelm Port Mahon, the principal port and fortress. And they had at the time a fast and well equipped fleet in the area.

FOURTH VOICE May18[th], 1756

2SL

At 9pm, a brisk northerly breeze sprang up and the squadron left Gibraltar and sailed through the night.

FOURTH VOICE May 19th. Daybreak

2SL

And the fleet sighted Minorca. The Castle of St Philips was under heavy French attack, but was still showing the British flag.

(2SL uses pointer)

Byng sent three ships to reconnoitre the mouth of Port Mahon Harbour to pick up the intelligence and to try to send a letter to General Blakeney commanding the Garrison to let him know, as Byng put it -

BYNG

That the fleet was here for his assistance. Although everyone was of opinion we could be no use to him. By all accounts, no place was secured for covering a landing - could we have spared any people.

2SL

A young Captain, the Honourable Augustus Hervey and later a very loyal friend of Byng, tried to communicate with St Philip's Castle. But when the enemy fleet appeared, that small detachment had to be recalled. That evening, there was manoeuvring between the two fleets, but still no engagement.

BYNG

With little wind, it was five o'clock before I could form my line or distinguish any of the enemy's motions. And I could not at all judge of their force save by their numbers, which was seventeen: and thirteen appeared large.

They first stood towards us on a regular line and tacked about seven. We tacked off towards the enemy at eleven.

FOURTH VOICE May 20th. Daybreak

2SL

Two smaller French ships appeared and were chased by the British: one was taken - one escaped. Four officers and a hundred and two private soldiers were taken, recent reinforcements once the French had spotted the British fleet.

The weather had been hazy that early morning and then later the enemy came into sight in the South East. By eleven o'clock, they were about six miles apart.

Two weeks before, Byng had drawn up a Line of Battle for the thirteen fighting ships which, by then, he had under his command. On the Starboard, as Admiral of the Blue, he would command the front section, the Van, from the

Ramillies. The largest ship with a complement of seven hundred and eighty men.

THIRD VOICE

Vice Admiral West, Admiral of the Red, would command the Rear from the *Buckingham.* Complement – five hundred and fifty three men.

2SL

In order, the first seven in the Van were to be -

SECOND VOICE *[seated]*

- the *Kingston* – under Captain William Parry

- the *Deptford* – under Captain John Amherst

- the *Culloden* – under Captain Henry Ward

- the *Ramillies* with Byng on board and Captain Gardiner, Flag Captain beside him

- the *Trident* – under Captain Philip Durell

17

- the *Princess Louise* – under Captain Thomas Noel

- and lastly the *Revenge* – under Captain Frederick Cornwall

2SL

In the *Rear*, 6 ships. In order

THIRD VOICE *[seated]*

- the *Intrepid* – under Captain James Young

- a ship called the *Captain* under Captain Charles Catford

- the *Buckingham* with Vice Admiral West on board and commanded by Captain Michael Everitt

- the *Lancaster* - under Captain The Honourable George Edgecombe

- the *Portland* – under Captain Patrick Baird - and lastly

- the *Defiance* – under Captain Thomas Andrew

2SL

On the other tack, the order would be exactly reversed.

By the time of battle, that was the position - so that the *Defiance* led the Van, including Admiral West in the *Buckingham* and Byng was in the Rear - with the *Kingston* the last in line.

The French fleet were twelve sail in a line of battle to leeward – with main topsails to the mast. ['square']

Essentially the French hove to – stopped – and waited to be attacked. Then they would aim at the rigging, seek to disable and move away at greater speed.

BYNG

The enemy now began to appear from the masthead. I called in the cruisers and when they had joined me, I tacked towards the enemy and formed the line ahead. I found the French were preparing theirs to leeward, having unsuccessfully endeavoured to weather me. They were just twelve large ships of the line and five frigates.

As soon as I judged the rear of fleet to be the length of their van, we tacked together and immediately I made the signal for the ships that led to lead large - and for the *Deptford* to quit the line, so that ours might become equal in number with theirs. At two o'clock I made the signal to engage.

2SL

But when Admiral Byng made that signal, the fleets were not parallel and formed an angle of 30 to 40°. So any attack was made worse by the distance between the two Rears being much greater than the Vans.

That is how Captain James Gilchrist, on an accompanying frigate called the *Experiment* saw it -

THIRD VOICE

Our Van bore down and engaged the enemy - and came in a parallel line with them. Our Rear went down angling upon the enemy. And therefore they could not all engage the enemy so near as the van did.

2SL

In other words, the Admiral's whole line could not come into action at the same moment. So when that signal to engage was made, the Van ran towards the French - so as to be approaching nearly head on. That meant they sacrificed their artillery fire. There were three raking broadsides and most of the Van ships were seriously damaged.

Then early on, the uniformity of the line was badly disturbed.

BYNG

The *Intrepid* unfortunately at the beginning had his foretopmast shot away. The Captain had no command of his ship. So he drove onto the ship next in and obliged that ship and the ships ahead of me to throw back. This obliged me to do so also for some minutes, to avoid their falling on board of me. Though not before we had drove our adversary out of the line.

2SL

So Byng ordered the *Chesterfield* to stand by the damaged *Intrepid* and the *Deptford* to take the *Intrepid's* place. And here the French tactics came into play.

BYNG

I found the enemy edged away constantly. As they went three feet to our one, they would never permit closing with them, but took the advantage of destroying our rigging.

2SL

During all this, there came a crucial moment for Admiral Byng.

Remember – as Byng had borne down on the French fleet at an angle, his leading ships had joined battle unsupported by the rest of his line. His Flag Captain, Captain Gardiner pointed out a solution to Byng.

SECOND VOICE *(stand)*

Sir, if you let the *Ramillies* stand out of the line - and move towards the enemy, we can bring the centre of the enemy to closer action. Then, with respect, Sir, the other ships in the Rear can follow suit.

2SL

But Byng refused to do it. He stuck rigidly to agreed naval tactics of the day. He recalled a Court martial where he had been a member and what then had happened to an earlier commander, Thomas Mathews, when he had chosen to take such action and had been roundly condemned.

BYNG *(stand)*

You see, Captain Gardiner that the signal for the line is out

(points to signal)

and that I am ahead of the *Princess Louise* and the *Trident*. And you would not have me as Admiral of the Fleet run down as if I was going to engage a single ship. It was Mr Matthew's misfortune to be prejudiced by not carrying his Force down together, which I shall endeavour to avoid.

SECOND VOICE As you will, Sir. *(Both sit)*

2SL

Byng wanted, however, to move towards the enemy and bravely, to hold his fire until his ships were at close range. As I said, Byng may have been an unadventurous Commander in Chief. Yet he was no coward.

But the battle itself became indecisive. However the English van, separated from the Rear, continued to get the brunt of the French guns.

Much time was spent later in analysing why the Rear did not become properly engaged. It is true that the **Ramillies** was fired on and also fired back - but at a greater distance than Byng desired. Indeed their opening fire came without orders, as some below deck became impatient. The Admiral then decided to let firing continue.

And Byng also suffered one handicap that he could not have foreseen. You have to imagine the smoke of battle everywhere and moments of no visibility at all. Suddenly the *Trident*, which should have been behind in the Rear, appeared on the lee bow.

THIRD VOICE *(reasonably loud)*   Look out!

But for the senior army officer, Lord Robert Bertie, spotting the ship so close, the *Trident* might have been fired upon in the belief that it was a French vessel. Byng had to order emergency avoiding action, all of which meant the enemy went further away.

So Byng's signals and the sails he ordered to be deployed all later came under considerable scrutiny, as did his own demeanour in battle.

Much time was spent on the 17th and 19th Articles of the Fighting Instructions, but we need not enter that territory. There is a much broader point to be made.

At that time, the highest Naval conception of a fleet action was of a dozen naval duels occurring simultaneously. Each ship against a separate opponent. Such a concept initially puts the attackers under a disadvantage. The Defenders can wait and choose their moment to fire. We have to wait for Rodney, Howe and

Nelson for more sophisticated and adventurous plans of battle.

So Byng must be judged by the tactics of the day. The unity of the line was paramount and woe betide the Commander who ignored it.

BYNG

By this time it was past six o'clock and the enemy's van and ours were at too greater distance to engage. I brought to about eight that night, to join the *Intrepid* and to refit our ships as fast as possible and continued so all night

2SL

Here the losses in killed and wounded were nearly equal on each side, but the British ships suffered much more than the French in the damage to masts and rigging. But Captain Andrews of the *Defiance* and Captain Noel of the *Princess Louisa* both lost their lives.

BYNG

The next morning we saw nothing of the enemy, though we were still lying to. Port Mahon was North North West about ten or eleven leagues.

2SL

Byng now called a Council of War of his remaining commanders and senior military men.

BYNG

Gentlemen, there are important matters to resolve.

2SL

They reached unanimously the following five conclusions:

FIRST VOICE

An attack on the French fleet will give no prospect of relieving Port Mahon. ['Marne']

SECOND VOICE

Even if there is no French fleet cruising at Minorca, the British Fleet cannot raise the siege.

FIRST VOICE

Gibraltar will be in danger if any Accident befalls the fleet.

SECOND VOICE

An attack by the British Fleet in its present state upon the French will also endanger Gibraltar and expose the trade in the Mediterranean to great hazards.

FIRST VOICE

It is in His Majesty's service that the Fleet shall proceed immediately to Gibraltar.

2SL

And that is what happened. The squadron repaired as much damage as it could en route. So the heart of it was a sober professional judgement:

THIRD VOICE

As the enemy is much superior in the weight of his metal and in the number of his men, it is not practical to relieve the fortress of St Philips.

2SL

And that, may I remind you all, is why officers under the Crown are trained. To make responsible calculations about the men under their command. For their lives are in your hands.

At the Rock, Byng found some reinforcements which had been sent to him. On May 25th, he had sent a full dispatch to the Admiralty. But that account was only published late - on June 26th - in a deliberately shortened form in the London Gazette. Omitted was his reference to sending the Resolutions of the Council of War and his key words about their discussions:

BYNG

In that Council of War, there was not the least dispute or doubt which arose amongst us.

2SL

It was a very fair point. And also unfairly omitted from the news report was his plea for reinforcements. As the Newgate Calender later put it -

THIRD VOICE

Every expression tending in any way to cast blame on the Ministers was 'carefully expunged.'

2SL

The politicians and their friends in the media had covered their backs. Sounds familiar? So the general public in their anger did not have the full picture which Byng had sought to paint. He – as the unsuccessful Commander in Chief remained the scapegoat. The public was incensed.

FOURTH VOICE

My brother's effigy was burned in public – such was the strength of feeling.

2SL

Of course, on Minorca, feelings had changed from elation to despair. Joyous when the English fleet first appeared in sight. Despair when the French fleet finally returned to its old station off Port Mahon.

That left General Sir William Blakeney to try to carry out resistance on Minorca. For seventy one days, heroically he held out, with a force of about five thousand, inflicting heavy losses on his attackers. Finally -

FOURTH VOICE
June 29th. The town of Port Mahon surrenders. General Blakeney capitulates on honourable terms to the Duke of Richelieu. The garrison is sent back to England.

2SL

In France and throughout the French dominions, there was huge public rejoicing. In England, shock, humiliation, grief and anger. King George the Second was outraged. The Duke of Newcastle in a blind panic. And in Admiral Byng - an obvious target for the popular resentment.

Those were the circumstances in which Admiral Sir Edward Hawke and Admiral Saunders were dispatched to Gibraltar to supersede Admirals Byng and West.

Ironically West in the *Buckingham* had engaged the French himself with huge commitment during the engagement, as Byng reported back to the Admiralty. But West had not had the support of the ships at the rear.

Both men were placed under arrest and taken back to England. It was however Admiral Byng who faced a Court Martial. And Admiral West was to give evidence, as the first witness.

MUSIC – Cue 3

SCENE 3 A – Court Martial

FIRST VOICE *(Stand after music fades-)*

Article 12 of the Articles of War – 1749 *(Sit)*

THIRD VOICE *(Stand)*

Every Person in the Fleet, who through cowardice, negligence, or disaffection shall in time of action withdraw, keep back, or not come into the fight or engagement, or shall not do his utmost to take or destroy every ship which it shall be his duty to engage-

and to assist and relieve all and every of His Majesty ships or those of his allies, which it shall be his duty to assist or relieve,

every such persons so offending and being convicted thereof by the sentence of a court martial - shall suffer death. *(Sit)*

2SL

So there was no room for manoeuvre on conviction. This Article of War had superseded one which had included after the word, 'Death' - the mitigating words –

THIRD VOICE

'or such other punishment as the circumstances of the offence shall deserve.'

2SL

That had allowed leniency to be exercised and frequently it was.
But not here.

FOURTH VOICE

December 27th 1756. The Court Martial of Admiral John Byng. On board the St George in Portsmouth Harbour.

2SL

Presiding: Vice-Admiral Thomas Smith. With Charles Fearne as Judge Advocate. Other members of the Court - Rear Admiral Francis Holburne, Harry Norris and Thomas Broderick and nine captains. They included Captain the Honourable Augustus Keppel, who was also a Member of Parliament. Byng was unrepresented.

FIRST VOICE *(Stand, as does Byng)*

John Byng - you face two charges.

First, under the Articles of War - that you did not do your utmost to destroy the ships of the French King, as was your duty - and further that you did not assist to your utmost your own fighting ships.

Second – that you did not do your utmost to relieve St Philip's Castle on His Majesty's Island of Minorca.

How do you plead, Sir?

BYNG

Not Guilty. *(Sits)*

2SL

The First was a Capital Charge. The Second a Misdemeanor.

On conviction, it would carry shame and disgrace. But not a sentence of Death.

FIRST VOICE - COURT

Call Vice Admiral Temple West

Do you swear by Almighty God to tell the truth, the whole truth and nothing but the truth?

SECOND VOICE – WEST *(Standing)*

I do.

FIRST VOICE *(Stand)]*

When did you first get sight of Minorca?

SECOND VOICE - WEST

On the 19th of May in the morning.

Q When did you first see the French fleet?

WEST

About noon on the 19th.

Q On the 20th, at what time were they formed and brought to?

WEST

I believe about one o'clock

Q At that time, how was our fleet standing and at what distance was your ship from the French?

WEST

Our fleet was standing in a regular formed line on the starboard tack and I think when our rear weathered their van, my ship might be about two miles distance from them.

Q How did the Admiral's ship and the rest of our fleet proceed from the time of our vans beginning to engage until the time the engagement was over?

WEST

At the time of the signal being made for engaging, I bore away for the enemy. They fired upon us as we were going down. I did not therefore, after that, know anything of the motions of the Rear division of the fleet - until the action with the enemy's Van had ceased.

Q But when you saw the Rear of the English fleet with the *Ramillies*, at a considerable distance astern from your ship, the *Buckingham*, what did you judge that distance to be?

SECOND VOICE - WEST

About 3 miles

Q Consider this, Sir. Did it appear to you that the wind and weather was such as to have permitted the Admiral and his Division to have got up with the enemy and engage them as close as the van did?

WEST

Yes, it appeared to me so. I knew of no impediment. I beg leave to observe that I don't say there was none, but that none appeared to me.

Q Frankly Sir, did you at any time see the Admiral and his division engage with the enemy?

WEST

I can only answer that by saying that I did see smoke from the Admiral's ship or from other ships of his division. I saw it as I was looking towards the *Intrepid*. But I was not able to discover at what ship the fire was directed.

Q Did you during the battle or afterwards express your opinion of the behaviour or proceedings of any of the officers or the ships? In particular, express any opinion of the behaviour or proceedings of the Admiral?

WEST

This question appears to me of an extraordinary nature!

I cannot conceive that, as a witness, I am at all called upon to know at what I expressed dissatisfaction. That is not a matter of fact.

But I will say this. When I saw the rear of our fleet astern, I could not but be dissatisfied with that appearance. I saw the fleet in that situation but cannot tell the reason. There was an appearance of some want in somebody, but with whom - I cannot pretend to say.

2SL

Next morning at the end of his examination in chief, West lifted the lid on the performance of other captains during the battle.

WEST

Going on board the Ramillies after the battle, I found Admiral Byng much dissatisfied with the behaviour of some of the ships in his division. I said I was very sorry to hear that and hoped if that was the case, he would not continue those captains in their command.

2SL

In fact, Admiral West had been extremely angry himself with three of them; Captains Parry, Ward and Cornwall in the *Kingston*, *Culloden* and *Revenge*. But they were not on trial. Byng cross - examined.

BYNG (*Rising*)

Did you not think it necessary to have
sufficient water and provisions on board for
this expedition - as it was known Minorca was
in enemy hands and consequently could not
supply anything?

WEST

I think so.

BYNG

When we reached Minorca, do you apprehend
that the enemy were masters of Mahon
Harbour?

WEST

The enemy were so far masters of the harbour
as to prevent the English fleet from making use
of it safely.

BYNG

Suppose that the land officers on board the
fleet could have been thrown into the castle of
St Philips. Do you consider it would have been
proper when the enemy's fleet was in sight?

WEST

The weakening of the force of the fleet would
have been highly inexcusable - by exposing the
English fleet to that of the enemy, who at that
time, in my opinion, was superior to it.

BYNG

Did you ever hear the Captains or any of the
officers of our fleet complain of their ships
being badly manned or sickly?

WEST

Yes. Many. *(Both sit)*

2SL

And then, ship by ship, Byng explored with Admiral West the state of repair of the vessels and whether they were deficient in their complement of men. Admiral West agreed and gave details of a plainly undermanned and less well equipped fleet than the French. So Admiral West had done his best to be loyal and fair to Byng.

But Byng, in his turn, had praised West after the battle–

BYNG

I want to thank you a thousand and a thousand times for your fine and gallant behaviour this day.

2SL

And when West's son had needed a surgeon, Byng had sent his own to attend to him.

Then to the stand came old General Lord Blakeney. Former Governor of Minorca and now created an Irish peer for his defence of St Philip's Castle.

FIRST VOICE

Is it your Lordship's opinion that the officers, men and recruits - about one hundred in all - said to have been on board the English fleet off Minorca - would have been of any considerable service in defending the Castle of St Philips, if they had been thrown into it?

THIRD VOICE - BLAKENEY

I am certain they would.

Q How much longer do you think the fort of St Philips might have held out if Lord Robert Bertie's Battalion had been thrown into it when the fleet was off Port Mahon?

BLAKENEY

There are so many incidents happening in war that it is a question which cannot be answered

2SL

But when cross-examined by Byng, the old soldier was a deadly witness.

BYNG

Do you consider that troops could have been landed safely from the fire of the enemy?

BLAKENEY

I have served sixty three years and I never knew yet any enterprise undertaken without some danger. And this might have been effected with as little

BYNG

Had the French any batteries opposite to the Castle at the time our fleet was off there?

BLAKENEY

Not at that time

BYNG

But Sir, is the night the proper time to land a body of men?

BLAKENEY

I know that I have landed in the night with men.

BYNG

Do you think - considering the situation of that harbour and the narrowness of its mouth - that men could be landed in the night without running any great hazard of being destroyed - or without even being seen by the enemy?

BLAKENEY

I believe there are gentlemen here who have seen the harbour and know it is not so very narrow at the landing places. And at this time, the enemy were in great want of ammunition and even fired stones. And these fell short.

2SL

So the elderly General left the witness box, having done real damage to Byng's case. He was supported by Robert Boyd, who had been storekeeper of the Ordnance at Minorca. Asked if those hundred soldiers would have been of service, Boyd replied-

BOYD / SECOND VOICE *(Stand)*

As we were much in want of officers and the duty was extremely hard upon those in garrison, the landing of that number must certainly have been of service to us.

FIRST VOICE - Call Captain Everett.

2SL

And Captain Everitt, who had commanded the *Buckingham*, fourth ship in the Van, was then sworn. He was a precise and balanced witness.

FIRST VOICE

Was there any unnecessary delay in the passage of the fleet from Gibraltar till you discovered the island of Minorca?

SECOND VOICE - EVERITT

Not as I know of
Q When did you get sight of Minorca?

EVERITT

At six o'clock in the morning of the 19th of May

Q At what time were you nearest to St Philips Castle and what distance from it?

EVERITT

About eleven o'clock in the forenoon and about two leagues distant

Q What time did you first see the French fleet that day?

EVERITT

The signal was made on seeing them about ten o'clock that morning, the 19th. About two o'clock in the afternoon they appeared to me standing to the westward. Our fleet was then standing to the South East.

Q Come now to the morning of the 20th. At what time did you first plainly see the French fleet?

EVERITT

At eight o'clock in the morning

Q What distance might our Van be from the French Van and our Rear from their Rear - at the time our Van first began to engage?

EVERITT

Our Van might be four hundred yards distance from theirs when we in the Van began to engage. I am not a competent judge of what distance our Rear was from their Rear. But they were at a much greater distance than we were.

Q How was the wind and weather - from the time seeing the French fleet in the morning till the action with them ended?

EVERITT

The wind was from the South South West and the weather very moderate.

Q So, could not the Rear of the fleet have come into action when the Van did? Or if not, then soon after?

EVERITT

I saw nothing to prevent it.

Q Do you remember any signals from the Admiral during the time of action?

EVERITT

Several. The first signal I saw was for a closer engagement with the enemy. That was at some time after three. Sometime after that, a signal was made for the Van of the fleet to stand on.

Q Was the signal for a closer engagement in general - or for a particular ship?

EVERITT

I understood it to be a general one.

Q Now, Captain Everitt, did you then see the Admiral ship engage with the enemy?

EVERITT *(Pause)*

I did not take any particular notice whether the fleet was engaged on not. And I can give no particular account of the position the Rear was in - during the time the Van was engaged.

Q But when the Van bore down to engage, upon the signal being made for battle, did the Rear division bear down on the same manner as the Van did?

EVERITT *(Pause)*

It appeared to me they did not.

Q Well Sir, did you then see the Admiral and our Rear make sail and use their utmost endeavours to intercept the Rear of the French and prevent their coming to you and giving their fire?

EVERITT

I saw them make some sail, but I don't know that they did their utmost.

Q When the signal was made for battle, did every ship in the English fleet bear down to attack the ship of the enemy he was opposed to - at a proper distance to engage her?

EVERITT

As our ship was pretty near in the centre of the Van, it seemed to me that every one of the Van went to the proper ship of the enemy opposed to her and engaged at the proper distance.

But the distance we were from the Rear would not allow me to judge so well what they did. Although it seemed to me they were a good deal further off from the enemy than the Van, in general, was.

Q Was the wind, weather and situation of the enemy such as would have enabled each ship to have done so?

EVERITT

I think so.

Q Captain Everrit, did you *ever* see the Admiral and his division engaged at a proper distance?

EVERITT

To the best of my remembrance, I saw the *Ramillies* firing, but it seemed to be a good distance off from the enemy.

Q What was the distance of our Van from the Van of the enemy and our Rear from their Rear - at the time the action began?

EVERITT

The distance of the Van was about two cables length or a little better from the enemy's. But that of our Rear from theirs seemed much more considerable.

Q Do you know of any reason why the Admiral and the Rear of our squadron did not engage as close as our Van?

EVERITT

If there was any, I was too busy then at my quarters to observe it.

Q If our Rear had made sail sooner, could they have cut off any or all of the French Rear and prevented them giving you their fire?

EVERITT

As that in a great measure depended on the sailing of our ships better than the French, and as I don't know that we had any trial as to who went best, I think I cannot resolve that question.

Q Finally, you have said that to the best of your memory, you saw the *Ramillies* firing. Do you remember what time that was?

EVERITT

I cannot speak with any certainty, but I think it was about a quarter of an hour after we began to engage.

FOURTH VOICE

Saturday, the first of January, 1758.

2SL

Admiral Byng requested that Lord Blakeney returned.
It was a crucial topic.

BYNG *(Stand)*

If the whole detachment had been landed at Minorca, could you have saved the island?

THIRD VOICE - BLAKENEY

'Tis impossible for anyone to tell that.

BYNG

Did Your Lordship never declare that even if that detachment ordered from Gibraltar had been landed, you could not have saved the island?

BLAKENEY

I have declared that, without force enough to drive the enemy from the island, there was no saving it.

2SL

The question was repeated.

BLAKENEY

By the oath I have taken, I believe I could have held out till Sir Edward Hawke came, if that detachment had been landed.

2SL

More damage. Then the first four lieutenants of Admiral West's own ship, the *Buckingham* gave evidence. All agreed that they did not know of any impediment to prevent Admiral Byng and his Division from coming to the assistance of the Van, which was closely engaged and raked by the enemy's rear as they came up. They also agreed that they did not see Byng go to a close engagement with the enemy.

FIRST VOICE

Captain Everett to be recalled. Captain Everitt, you are still under oath. Admiral Byng has some questions for you.

2SL

And this time Byng was more successful. He began with the failure to try to relieve Minorca.

BYNG

Supposing the land forces on board the fleet could have been thrown into St Philips Castle. Do you consider it would have been proper when the enemy's fleet was in sight?

SECOND VOICE - EVERITT

I think it would not

BYNG

Do you consider that if the land forces had been thrown in to reinforce the garrison, that the ships would have been fit for action and fit to engage the enemy's fleet?

EVERITT

They would not have been fit to engage then.

BYNG

Do you think that throwing in about a hundred officers and recruits as a reinforcement to the garrison of the Castle of St Philips would have been a force sufficient to have enabled it to hold out against the enemy's attacks?

EVERITT

I don't know that it would

BYNG

Did you ever hear the Captains or other officers
of the fleet complain of their ships being badly
manned and sickly?

EVERITT

I believe I did

BYNG

Captain Everitt, I want to come to the time
when the rear of the French passed you. Was
the Van of our fleet then in a condition to
pursue them?

EVERITT

I believe they were not

BYNG

Do you apprehend that it would have been
proper to pursue the enemy with *part* of the
fleet?

EVERITT

I don't know that it would

BYNG

You have said that when the rear of the French fleet passed our van, the van was not in a condition to pursue, as you believe. What were your reasons for believing that?

EVERITT

Many had their sails and rigging much cut. The *Buckingham's* main topsail yard had gone. That, I believe, was the reason that they could not pursue them.

2SL

Who could convict on that evidence?

FIRST VOICE

Captain Lloyd, please

2SL

This witness captained a supporting ship, the *Chesterfield* which was not in the line of battle. But it was close enough to be able to describe in detail Byng's own ship, the *Ramillies* having to back her topsail in order to avoid a collision with the *Trident*.

THIRD VOICE - LLOYD

The *Trident* seemed to be close under the lee bow and they appeared to me as if they were on board each other.

2SL

A crucial point. For if Byng was to be convicted of 'not doing his utmost', then it had to be shown that there was no good reason for the *Ramillies* stopping when she did - and no reason for Byng having to command the rest of the ships in the line to stop as well

He was questioned in detail by the Court about Byng. How much sail had his ships set? Captain Lloyd became angry.

FIRST VOICE

You seem to be warm Sir, which is not becoming.

THIRD VOICE - LLOYD

I am not warm, but it behoves me to see that my evidence is consistent!

2SL

But Captain Lloyd stuck to his guns and made it clear that it was necessary for the *Ramillies* to take swift action to avoid a collision. Byng had no choice.

FIRST VOICE

Captain James Young

2SL

Captain of the *Intrepid* – Last ship in line in the Van, which had been replaced in the line after the fore topmast had been shot away. Potentially a valuable witness for the prosecution, as an early question made clear

FIRST VOICE - COURT

Did the loss of your fore topmast put any ship in danger of being on board of you?

THIRD VOICE – YOUNG

No, not that I could perceive at all.

FIRST VOICE

Did the loss of your fore topmast cause any impediment to the Admiral and the Rear division so as to prevent them from going down and engaging the enemy closely?

THIRD VOICE - YOUNG

Not that I could perceive

FIRST VOICE

When the signal was made for battle, what ships of ours first steered down for the enemy?

THIRD VOICE - YOUNG

I put myself right before the wind, as I saw Rear Admiral West and the rest of that division do.

FIRST VOICE - COURT

Captain, please now recall the wind at that time. Now if the Admiral and his Division had set all their sails from the time the signal was made to battle and bore away properly, *could they have come to a close engagement with the enemy?*

THIRD VOICE - YOUNG

Yes. They were lying to for us. I went down only under my topsails.

FIRST VOICE – COURT

Did you see the Admiral and his Division engaged at all?

THIRD VOICE - YOUNG

Yes, some of the ships did fire.

FIRST VOICE - COURT

But were they ever within point-blank of the enemy?

THIRD VOICE - YOUNG

I can't judge that.

FIRST VOICE - COURT

Were not our ships in a line of battle, ahead of one another, when the signal was made to engage?

THIRD VOICE - YOUNG

Yes, they were in a very good line.

FIRST VOICE – COURT

But were not our ships in an oblique line with that of the enemy - with the two Rears forming the greatest distance from each other?

THIRD VOICE - YOUNG

To be sure, the two Rears were at the greatest distance from each other, because our Rear was to windward of our Van.

FIRST VOICE - COURT

In the position the two lines were in, was it possible to bring on a *general* action without the Admiral in the Rear Division going right before the wind upon the enemy and carrying more sail than the Van did?

THIRD VOICE - YOUNG

No, there was no possibility of a general engagement, without *all* going down and the sail made proportioned to the going of the ships.

FIRST VOICE – COURT

Now you have said hitherto that it was not much above three quarters of an hour or an hour before the Admiral and the Rear division passed by your ship, the *Intrepid*. Did you see any impediment which prevented the English Rear division from passing sooner and engaging the enemy - according to the signal which was then flying?

THIRD VOICE - YOUNG

No, nothing at all appeared to me. That is, if they had had the same wind and weather that I had.

FIRST VOICE – COURT

How many men did you have killed or wounded?

THIRD VOICE – YOUNG

It was ten, I think, that were killed outright that day. And forty wounded. About six or seven of the wounded men died in our passage down.

BYNG *(Rising to cross-examine)*

Captain Young, what was the condition of your ship when you joined me at Spithead?

THIRD VOICE - YOUNG

She was, I thought, in very bad repair. Indeed I had complained to you when I joined you that her ports had all been very bad.

BYNG

Had you any powder damaged by taking in so much water at her ports?

THIRD VOICE - YOUNG

By the leaking of the ship and thus the water we took in, the ground tier of powder was all damaged. And when we arrived at Gibraltar, she was condemned as unserviceable.

BYNG

And how was your ship manned?

THIRD VOICE - YOUNG

Indifferently. She had her number when she came out. But soldiers were included as part of the complement.

BYNG

Did you form any judgement of the enemy's force? Did you believe them to be superior to the British fleet, either before or after the action?

THIRD VOICE - YOUNG

By what judgement I can make of ships, I thought them to be our match, if not more.

BYNG

As you have said that you did not see the *Revenge* from the time that you lost your fore topmast until she was near you and did not know where she was, *how do you know* that there was no impediment to our Rear closing the enemy during that time?

THIRD VOICE -YOUNG

I - I answered as to my own ship - that *I* made no impediment to any other ships closing. That is all that appeared to me.

2SL

It was a good question and Captain Young's qualified answer undid some of the damage.

FIRST VOICE - COURT

You have said that your ship was indifferently manned. How did your men behave on the 20th of May during the action?

THIRD VOICE - YOUNG

When I said that, I meant as to numbers of Seamen. But those that were in her, behaved in the action as well as any of the best Seaman could do.

Next, Captain Cornwall of the *Revenge*, the ship immediately behind the *Intrepid.* Potentially, this witness was in a difficult position. When the *Intrepid* had been damaged, he brought up his ship and engaged his French opposite number, he said for half an hour, expecting any minute that Admiral Byng would signal the *Intrepid* to leave the line.

SECOND VOICE – CORNWALL

Because the *Intrepid* was the cause that I could not go on.

But on waiting some time------ My Lords, what I have to tell may be against myself. But as I am sworn to tell the truth, I must do so.

Having waited some time, I thought it might be for the King's service to endeavour to go on. So I closed with the *Intrepid* - almost within the fire of her guns. When I was there, I had great reason to apprehend I might have been becalmed alongside. So I sent a boat to Captain

Young to tell him that I thought it was for our service to go up to the relief of the Van.

2SL

In other words, this Captain had broken away from the line of battle and had born away with the Van towards the enemy. It had not pleased Byng.

FIRST VOICE - Q

You have said that you bore away when the van did. Tell the Court if the Admiral and the rest of the Rear did so?

SECOND VOICE - CORNWALL

I can't recollect that I saw the Admiral or any of the ships until the time that I told the Court before – when I looked out.

Q Was the fleet in a line of battle when the signal was made to engage?

SECOND VOICE - CORNWALL

They were in a line of battle, but the Rear of the fleet was at a greater distance from the enemy than the Van was.

Q Captain Cornwall, please now remember the considerable distance between the leading ship of our Van and the leading ship of theirs. Now was there any way for each ship of our Rear to have engaged his opponent?

SECOND VOICE - CORNWALL

Had every ship made a proportioned similar sail and so bore down together, I should think there could not have been any great difference in their coming down. But the Captains who commanded the ships are certainly the best judges of that matter. They could best tell what they could do in their own situations.

Q Did the enemy shot strike the *Revenge*?

SECOND VOICE - CORNWALL

The shot reached the *Revenge,* but we were never very near the enemy. I do not think we were within musket shot, because I never suffered a musket to be fired.

Q What number of men were killed and wounded in the action?

SECOND VOICE - CORNWALL

Only five wounded. None killed.

BYNG *(Rising)*

Let me come first to your own ship's complement. How was your ship manned two days before the action?

SECOND VOICE - CORNWALL

She was very indifferently manned as to seamen, which I represented to the Admiral, I believe the day before the action.

BYNG

How many men had you on board then?

SECOND VOICE - CORNWALL

I can't be positive, but I believe seventy or about.

BYNG

Was not a reinforcement of thirty men ordered from the *Phoenix* on the evening before the action, on your application to me of her being an ill manned ship and very sickly?

SECOND VOICE - CORNWALL

Yes, it was.

BYNG

Finally this, Captain Cornwall. What does the 24th Article of the general sailing and fighting Instructions direct a captain to do when in a line of battle? –

SECOND VOICE - CORNWALL

To keep in his station in the line and close up the line.

FIRST VOICE - COURT

This court has nothing to do with Captain Cornwall's duty

2SL

Maybe, but you can sense in Byng's question a reproof to the Captain for his own independent actions.

Then at last, an important witness for Admiral Byng. Lord Robert Bertie, a soldier who had been alongside him throughout. Byng questioned him shrewdly

BYNG

Did you observe that the castle of St Phillips was besieged?

THIRD VOICE - BERTIE

Yes I did.

BYNG

Do you consider that the throwing in of about a hundred men, consisting of officers and recruits would have enabled the Castle to hold out against the enemy's attacks?

THIRD VOICE - BERTIE

No, I consider that they would be of much more use on board the Fleet.

BYNG

Were you on the quarterdeck near me during the whole time of the enemy's firing?

THIRD VOICE - BERTIE

Yes, the whole time.

BYNG

At that time when the enemy was firing on us and their shots, passing over us, did your Lordship hear me say anything?

THIRD VOICE - BERTIE

[Turning to the Court] I recollect when the French began to fire on us, that the Admiral desired Captain Gardiner not to fire until such time as we were close alongside of them.

BYNG

What did your Lordship inform me during the time of firing?

THIRD VOICE - BERTIE

I said - do you or Captain Gardiner see that ship upon our starboard bow? I think it to be one of ours, and if you don't take great care, we shall fire into her. Afterwards, the Admiral desired me to go down to the lower deck and endeavour to stop them from firing.

(To the Court) I would say this to the Court. In general, I was near to the Admiral the whole day of the action. He seemed to me to give his orders coolly and distinctly, and I do not apprehend that he was in the least wanting in personal courage.

FIRST VOICE - COURT

So My Lord, did the Admiral appear solicitous to engage the enemy and assist His Majesty's ships that were engaged with the enemy?

THIRD VOICE - BERTIE

(Firmly) Yes. He did.

Q Lastly, did Your Lordship on or after the day of action hear any murmuring or discontent among the officers or men upon any supposition that the Admiral had not done his duty?

THIRD VOICE - BERTIE

I never heard anyone of the *Ramillies* speak the least disrespectfully of the Admiral. Or ever hint that the Admiral had not done his duty.

2SL

And Colonel Marcus Smith, who was also on the quarter deck with the Admiral, confirmed exactly what Lord Robert Bertie had said.

SECOND VOICE - COL SMITH

I did not see any backwardness or marks of fear or confusion. Rather the reverse, I thought. The Admiral gave his orders very coolly and without the least confusion

2SL

So yet again - Admiral Byng was no coward. Indeed Captain Gardiner of the *Ramillies*, recalled by Byng at the end of proceedings, told the Court that Admiral Byng showed quite the reverse of fear and there was nothing to allege against his personal behaviour. That was brought out fairly before the Court.

FIRST VOICE - COURT

Did you perceive any backwardness in the Admiral during the action or any marks of fear or confusion, either from his countenance or behaviour?

SECOND VOICE - GARDINER

I did not.

Q Did the Admiral gave his orders with calmness, and as quick as the nature of things would admit – or did he appear confused in giving his orders?

SECOND VOICE - GARDINER

He seemed to me to give his orders clearly and explicitly.

Q Did the Admiral appear solicitous to engage the enemy, and to assist His Majesty's ships that were engaged with the enemy?

SECOND VOICE - GARDINER

I think he did.

Q And did you on or after the day of action hear any murmuring or discontent among the Officers or Men on the *Ramillies* on any supposition that the Admiral had not done his duty ?

SECOND VOICE - GARDINER

I did not.

FIRST VOICE - COURT *(Stands)*

The Court stands adjourned until tomorrow morning.

All cast stand, bow as if to a Judge and exit as directed

Music - Cue 5

INTERVAL

SCENE 3 B

2SL

Denied the aid of counsel by the practice then of Courts Martial, Admiral Byng set out his own case in writing. Suffering from an eye infection, he asked that the Judge Advocate should read it to the Court.

Let part of it be the final speech that he did not make.

BYNG *(Stands)*

It is my misfortune to have laboured under the disadvantage of a popular and almost national prejudice.

It has been echoed throughout the Kingdom that the loss of St Phillip's Castle was certainly owing to my misconduct and that Minorca might have been relieved if I had done my duty.

As this national calamity has been urged in order to excite a national reproach against me, I must beg leave to refute this assertion.

And should this part of the accusation be once clearly answered and the prejudice removed, certain I am that the charge of personal cowardice in the action will soon vanish.

It may seem somewhat singular that being accused of two offences, one of which is capital and the other not, I should appear more solicitous to acquit myself of that which is only a misdemeanour - than of that which directly affects my life.

But permit me to say I still retain so just a sense of the value of my honour - as to prefer Death to the disgrace that ought to attend the author of so inglorious a calamity to his country.

So if then I can acquit myself of this imputation - which I am confident I can - I shall, with spirit, proceed to my defence against the charge of Cowardice and treat it with the contempt it deserves.

2SL

In the first part of his Defence, Byng set out to satisfy the Court that he did the utmost in his power to relieve Minorca. But he added an important qualification -

BYNG

In order to determine whether I did my utmost - I say that the consideration of what I *could* do should take precedence over any determination of what I *ought* to have done.

Let me lay it down as an undeniable fact, which I shall prove: that the French fleet was superior in the size of their ships, weight of metal and number of men - besides their advantage in point of sailing - which enabled them to fight or avoid fighting as best suited their purposes.

Yet you will find, by letter to me from the Admiralty, that the only reason pretended for dismissing me from my command was *'retreating from an inferior force.'*

Now instead my retreating from an inferior force, *a superior force retreated from me, when the fleet was unable to pursue.*

2SL

And now Byng asked a crucial question - with what intention had he been sent out on this ill - fated expedition?

BYNG

If it be answered – 'To protect or relieve Minorca' - which is the seeming language of my instructions, I would again ask -- did those who sent me consider that Minorca could be invaded before my arrival?

Did they consider that when they sent me out with so inadequate a force? If they did, their conduct is unjustifiable. If they did not, their ignorance is inexcusable.

This, I presume, is sufficient to unravel the political secret - why the enemy's force has been so industriously lessened and mine so extravagantly magnified.

In these Instructions, you will find I am ordered that -

FIRST VOICE *(Seated)*

'If on your arrival at Gibraltar, the French fleet should have passed out of the Mediterranean, you are to send a detachment under the command of Admiral West after them to North America.'

BYNG

Now can it be meant that I was to detach eight ships out of the ten I then had - as no less than ten would have been necessary to ensure success - and make the superior force ordered in my instructions? Again I am ordered –

FIRST VOICE

'When arriving at Minorca, you are to assist the garrison with Lord Robert Bertie's regiment and as many gunners and men as you can spare out of the fleet.'

BYNG

Does this not suppose the sea to be open and the fleet unopposed? Otherwise the order would be absurd. For how could it be expected that I should disarm the squadron, by sending part of its proper complement – which, please observe, the Fusiliers were – on shore, when the whole was too little to secure success at sea? I am further ordered –

FIRST VOICE

"If Minorca is not attacked, you are to block up Toulon."

BYNG

Toulon, where the French fleet was harboured.

What - block up a superior fleet with an inferior fleet?

Does not all this show that fighting was the least intentional part of my instructions - and that if the Admiralty had expected an engagement, is it not to be supposed that they would have sent more ships?

So under these unfavourable circumstances, without such intelligence of the Enemy's force as could enable me to judge it - and determined to do my duty - I took command of the squadron, such as it was.

Many ships were foul and one, in particular, the *Intrepid,* reported unfit for the voyage. With these I proceeded as expeditiously as possible.

When I arrived at Gibraltar, I received intelligence that a landing had been actually made on the island of Minorca! The harbour and the whole island was in the enemy's possession, except the Castle of Saint Philip, which was then besieged by a very considerable force on land.

And the siege was covered by a strong squadron at sea, superior to mine.

Every person there in Gibraltar concluded the place was lost. I must own there appeared to me no great probability of preserving Minorca at this time.

Thus far, I will presume upon my innocence, but why, it may be asked, was not Minorca relieved at this time?

I answer *because I was not sent in enough time to prevent the enemy landing.*

And that when I was sent, *I was not strong enough to beat the enemy's fleet and raise the siege.*

Let others answer why I came so late and why I came so weak with a force not calculated for such an expedition. That is my answer.

2SL

Byng then faced up to two crucial questions.

First - why after the engagement – he did not attack the enemy?

Second - why he did not land the help that he had on board.

BYNG

I might, indeed, have done the first, with the certainty almost of being defeated. I could not have done the second, even if I had been victorious.

And had I been defeated, what refuge would have been left for the shattered fleet? What security for Gibraltar?

Gibraltar, which then must have been exposed to the hazard of a sudden siege, without a single ship to defend it. For remember, that place was equally recommended to my protection.

For this issue is raised by these proceedings: indeed it is the very heart of it: *Is a Commander expected to fight in all situations and under all disadvantages?*

Surely such extremes are culpable. Where nothing is to be gained and all may be lost, Fighting becomes presumptuous rashness or frenzy.

I therefore beg leave to recommend to your particular consideration the different situations of the two fleets at this time. And I refer you again to the minutes of that Council of War held on board the *Ramillies* on the 24th of May, which has already been laid before the court.

2SL

Then Byng turned to the second part of the charge against him. He began with the 12th Article of War.

He argued that in order to bring any person within this Article, he had to be convicted of cowardice, negligence or disaffection. And Negligence could not be taken so broadly as to mean every sort of neglect and omission but only Gross Negligence. For that, he accepted, would indicate also Cowardice or Disaffection.

So he argued that only Gross Negligence could have been intended to make a capital offence.

BYNG

Any other construction might expose the bravest man that ever commanded to the severest penalties, since a single error in judgment might render him liable to the most capital punishment.

By this rule, I must desire my conduct may be judged. And if my intentions appear to be good, and my courage clear, I ought to stand acquitted by all good men, even though my abilities should be deemed deficient.

And I ask the Court never to forget that no Commander of a particular ship has a right to deviate from the established discipline and rules of the Navy, contained in the Fighting Instructions and founded on experience and just observation.

Because if inferior officers may judge for themselves, there is an end of all discipline and any deviation from Orders must tend to disturb and disconcert the Admiral's plan and throw the whole fleet into confusion.

I shall now proceed to lay before the Court a faithful narrative of the material transactions of His Majesty's fleet under my command off the island of Minorca from the 19th of May 1756 to the 24th... *(Sits)*

2SL

And Byng gave his detailed account of the days of action.

After which the Court retired to consider its verdict

Music – Cue 6

SCENE 4 - Finding, Sentence and Recommendation

FOURTH VOICE January 27th 1757

2SL

On their return, the Court had reached unanimously thirty seven conclusions. Five were critical of Admiral Byng. In essence, they decided -

FIRST VOICE *(stand)*

That Admiral John Byng did not do his utmost to relieve St Philips Castle.

And also that during the engagement between His Majesty's fleet and the fleet of the French king, on the 20th of May last, he did not do his utmost to take, sink, burn and destroy the ships of the French king, which it was his duty to have engaged, and to assist such of his Majesty's ships as were engaged.

We therefore unanimously agree that he falls under part of the 12th article of an Act of Parliament, of the 22nd year of His present Majesty.

And as that Article prescribes death, without any alternative left to the discretion of the Court under any variation of circumstance, the Court do thereby unanimously adjudge the said Admiral John Byng to be shot to death, at such time and on board such ship as the Lords Commissioners of the Admiralty shall direct.

SECOND VOICE *(Stand)*

But as it appears, by the evidence of Lord Robert Bertie, Lieutenant Colonel Smith, Captain Gardener, and other officers of the ship who were near the person of the Admiral, that they did not perceive any backwardness in him during the action, or any marks of fear or confusion, either from his countenance or behaviour –but that he seemed to give his orders coolly and distinctly and did not seem wanting in personal carriage and, from other circumstances,

- the Court do not believe that his misconduct arose either from cowardice or disaffection and do therefore unanimously think in their duty earnestly to recommend him as a proper object of mercy.

(First and Second Voices sit)

2SL

The Court went further, for when they sent a copy of their proceedings to the Board - they enclosed a letter which ended -

SECOND VOICE *(Stand)*

'We cannot help laying the distresses of our minds before your Lordships on this occasion, in finding ourselves under the necessity of condemning a man to death from the great severity of the 12th Article of War, part of which he falls under, and which admits of no mitigation,- even if the crime should be committed by an error in judgment.

And therefore, for our own conscience sake, as well as injustice to the prisoner, we pray your Lordships in the most earnest manner to recommend him to His Majesty's clemency.'
(Sit)

SCENE 5 – Opinion of the Judges

2SL

The Lord Commissioners of the Admiralty were more concerned about a question of law than mercy

THIRD VOICE *(Stand)*

'Doubts having arisen, with regard to the legality of the sentence, particularly whether the crime of negligence which is not expressed in any part of the proceedings can, in this case, be supplied by implication, we ask His Majesty King George The Second that the opinion of the Judges be taken whether the sentence was legal.' *(Sit)*

2SL

The Judges included Lord Mansfield and on February the 14th, 1757 – but without reasons - came the answer:

FIRST VOICE *(Seated)*

'We have considered the said sentence, together with the 12th Article therein referred to, and are unanimously of opinion that it is a legal sentence.'

2SL

So there was to be no legal loophole and no reprieve.

Pitt, then Foreign Secretary, had the courage and integrity to stand up against the public outcry against Byng. At a Cabinet Council on February 26th, he told the King that the House of Commons wanted Byng to be pardoned. To that the King memorably retorted:

THIRD VOICE - KING *(Seated)*

"Sir, you have taught me to look for the sense of my subjects in another place than the House of Commons."

SCENE 6 – Proceedings in Parliament

2SL

But Captain Keppel made a last effort to save Byng and got a temporary respite by stating in the House of Commons that he and other members of the Court Martial desired to be released from their oath of secrecy, that they might reveal the grounds on which they recommended Byng to mercy.

So a Bill was brought into the House of Commons for that purpose and it passed with little opposition. However when it was carried to the House of Lords, it was thrown out on the Second Reading. No technical device was going to frustrate the public anger. For public anger, then as now, must be dissipated, must it not?

On February 15th, the Board of Admiralty confirmed the sentence of Death. Admiral West resigned in protest.

SECOND VOICE - WEST

I will not choose to serve on terms which would subject another officer to the treatment shown to Admiral Byng.

SCENE 7 - Letter of BYNG'S Sister

2SL

The Honourable Mrs Sarah Osborne, Admiral Byng's sister - wrote to the Lords of the Admiralty

FOURTH VOICE *(Stand)*

'My Lords. The Judges having reported to his Majesty in Council that the sentence passed on my unfortunate brother is a legal one, permit me to implore your Majesty your Lordships' intercession with His Majesty for his most gracious mercy.

The court martial, My Lords, seems to have acquitted my unhappy brother of cowardice and disaffection and, therefore, it is presumed he stands sentenced under the head of negligence.

It is not fitting, perhaps, that a wretched woman, as I am, should offer any arguments in my brother's relief to your Lordships, who are masters of the whole. But what criminal negligence, My Lords, can there have been - in which neither cowardice nor disaffection have had a part?

Why, My Lords, should my poor brother suffer, when both the sentence by which he is condemned and a letter to your Lordships by which he is so strongly recommended to His Majesty's mercy, fully prove that his judges did not deem him deserving the punishment they thought themselves obliged to sentence him to?

For the reasons I have ventured briefly to offer, and the many others must that must occur to your Lordships, his case appears to be uncommonly *hard*, and well deserving that mercy to which his judges have so earnestly recommended him. I hope I shall stand excused if I beseech Your Lordships' immediate intercession with His Majesty on his behalf.

17th February 1757.'

Music – Cue 7

2SL

Sadly this perceptive and moving letter passed unheeded. And Byng refused chances to escape from custody. That had been suggested and investigated by Captain the Honourable Augustus Hervey, who as a good friend, had been making great efforts behind the scenes to try to save his life.

SCENE 8 - Pleas for Clemency

2SL

Two distinguished Frenchmen also tried to save him and it does them both great credit. The Duke of Richelieu was a Marshal of France and the successful invader of Minorca. Now in Paris after his stunning success in Minorca.

SECOND VOICE - Duke of Richelieu

Sir, I am very sensibly concerned for Admiral Byng. I do assure you whatever I have seen or heard of him does him honour. After having done all that man could reasonably expect from him, he ought not to be censured for suffering a defeat.

When two commanders contend for victory, though both are equally men of honour, yet one must necessarily be worsted. And all there is against Mr Byng is ...that he was worsted. For his whole conduct was that of an able seaman and is justly worthy of admiration.

The strength of our two fleets was the least equal: the English had thirteen ships and we had twelve – but we were much better equipped. Fortune that presides over all battles, and especially those that are fought at sea, fortune was more favourable to us than to our adversaries, by sending our shot into their ships with greater execution.

I am persuaded, and it is the generally received opinion, that if the English had obstinately continued the engagement, their whole fleet would have been destroyed.

In short, there can be no higher act of injustice than what is now attempted against Admiral Byng, and all men of honour, and all gentlemen of the army, are particularly concerned in the event.

2SL

Voltaire passed on this letter to Byng, adding -

THIRD VOICE - Voltaire

Honour, humanity and equity, order me to convey it into your hands. This noble and unexpected testimony from one of the most candid as well as the most generous of my countrymen, makes me presume your Judges will do you the same justice.

I am with respect, your most humble, obedient servant, *Voltaire.*

2SL

Two days before his death, Admiral Byng wrote a last letter to his sister Sarah

BYNG

My Dear, Dear Sister - I can only with my last breath thank you over and over again for all your endeavours to save me in my present situation. All has proved fruitless, but nothing wanting in you that could be done.

God forever bless you is the sincere prayer of your affectionate Brother, John Byng.

SCENE 9 - Death on a Quarter Deck

FOURTH VOICE *(Stand)]*

Sunday morning, March 13th, 1757. *(Sit)*

2SL

The warrant for Byng's execution next day was read to him. He was concerned at first to hear that the place appointed by the warrant was on the forecastle, where ordinary seaman would have met their fate.

BYNG *(Stand)*

Is not this an indignity to my birth, to my family and to my rank in the service? I think I have not been treated like an officer in any instance since I was disgraced - except in being ordered to be shot.

2SL

But then, comforted by his friends, Byng took hold of himself.

BYNG

It is very true, the place or manner is of no great importance to me. But I think living admirals should consult the dignity of their rank for their own sakes. I cannot plead a precedent. There is no precedent of an Admiral or a general officer in the army being shot. They make such a precedent of me that Admirals hereafter may feel the effects of it.

2SL

That Sunday at his last dinner, he was cheerful as usual and ordered that evening a small bowl of punch to be made and then raised his glass -

BYNG

My friends, here are your healths and God bless you all. I am pleased to find I have some friends still, notwithstanding my misfortunes.

2SL

Then he put down his glass - and added

BYNG

I am to die tomorrow. And as my country requires my blood - I am ready to resign it, though I do not as yet know what my crime is.

I think my judges, in justice to posterity and to officers who come after me, should have explained my crime a little more, and pointed out the way to avoid falling into the same error I did. As the sentence and resolutions now stand, I am persuaded no Admiral will be wiser hereafter by them or know better how to conduct himself on the like occasion.

FOURTH VOICE *(Stand – remain standing)*

Spithead. Monday March 14th, 1757.

2SL

Admiral Byng spent much of the morning by himself in the State Room of the ship the *Monarque.* Then he came down to a breakfast.

He wore a plain light grey suit - as he had since Gibraltar, when he was told of his suspension. Then he had taken off his uniform and thrown it into the sea.

FIRST VOICE *(Stand, remain standing)*

All the men at war at Spithead had orders to send their boats with the Captains and every officer of the ship and a party of Marines under arms to attend the execution.

SECOND VOICE *([Stand, remain standing)*

We reached the harbour just after 11 o'clock with great difficulty, as a gale was blowing.

The *Monarque* lay high and the sea ran high, but nonetheless a large number of boats gathered around it.

FIRST VOICE

Half an hour before he died, the Admiral's ship in the Mediterranean, the *Ramillies* was riding at her moorings in the harbour and broke her moorings chain. For some, it was an omen.

SECOND VOICE

Admiral Byng, accompanied by a clergyman and two relations, walked out of the Great Cabin to the Quarterdeck a few minutes before 12 o'clock. He was dressed in a light grey coat, white waistcoat, white stockings and a large white wig - *[pause]* - and he had in each hand a white handkerchief.

THIRD VOICE *(Stand, remain standing)*

From the beginning, he had said that he would not be blindfolded and that he alone would give the Marines the order to fire.

BYNG

As it is my fate, I can look at it and receive it.

THIRD VOICE

But shortly before his death, he was persuaded to wear a blindfold lest the young Marines in his firing squad - the nearest only two feet away - would be overawed and intimidated. For *their* sake, he relented.

BYNG

If it must be so, and you insist, it must be so.

2SL

Just before his execution, he delivered to William Brough, Marshal of the High Court of Admiralty, the following paper:

BYNG

Sir. These are my thoughts on this occasion.

Happy for me, at this my last moment, that I know my own innocence, and am conscious that no part of my country's misfortunes can be owing to me. I heartily wish the shedding my blood may contribute to the happiness and service of my country, but cannot resign my just claim to a faithful discharge of my duty, according to the best of my judgment - and the utmost exertion of my ability for His Majesty's honour and my country's service.

I am sorry that my endeavours were not attended with more success - and that the armament under my command proved too weak to succeed in an expedition of such a moment.

Truth has prevailed over calumny and falsehood and justice has wiped off the ignominious stain of my supposed want of personal courage or disaffection. My heart acquits me of these crimes.

But who can be presumptuously sure of his own judgment?

If my crime is an error in judgment, or differing in opinion from my judges – and if yet the error of judgment should be on their side, God forgive them, as I do. And may the distress of their minds and uneasiness of their consciences, which in justice to me they have represented, be relieved and subside, as my resentment has done.

The Supreme Judge sees all hearts and motives; and to him I must submit the justice of my cause.

John Byng. On board His Majesty's ship *Monarque*, in Portsmouth Harbour, March 14, 1757.

SECOND VOICE

He threw his hat on the deck and knelt on a cushion. A friend offered to tie the bandage over his eyes but he said

BYNG

I am obliged to you, sir. - I thank God I can do it myself –

I think I can -- I am sure I can.

SECOND VOICE

And he tied it behind his head himself. Then he dropped the other handkerchief as a signal - and six marines fired. Five bullets went through him and he died in an instant.

2SL

He died with a great resolution and composure without the slightest sign of fear. And when he fell, an ordinary seaman called out -

THIRD VOICE

'There lies the bravest officer in the Navy.'

(All sit, save 2SL)

SCENE 10 - To encourage the others

2SL

And that is how one naval officer died. In the cynical and famous words of **Voltaire**, he was put to death –

FOURTH VOICE ' *Pour encourager les autres'*

2SL

Yes - to encourage the others. As if they needed it.

Buried in the family crypt in a quiet village in Bedfordshire, some believe that Dr Samuel Johnson wrote for his monument this inscription:

THIRD VOICE *(Stand)*

"To the perpetual disgrace of public justice, the Hon John Byng Esquire, Admiral of the Blue, fell a martyr to political persecution, March 14th in the year 1757: when Bravery and Loyalty were insufficient securities for the Life and Honour of a Naval Officer." *(Sit)*

Music – Cue 9

2SL

His family continued to serve their country with distinction and honour.

FOURTH VOICE

Sarah, his sister, was widowed young. Her surviving son died whilst Governor of New York and Sarah brought up his two sons, one becoming a General and the second serving as the British Minister in Dresden. She was a woman of extraordinary courage, resilience and character, as her letter so clearly demonstrated.

FIRST VOICE The second Viscount Torrington, Paymaster General in Ireland.

SECOND VOICE Robert Byng, Commissioner of the Navy and Governor of Barbados.

THIRD VOICE: George Byng, Grandson: Member of Parliament in Middlesex for 56 years.

2SL

And Sir John Byng, a Field Marshal in the Army whose heroic conduct in many a battle and particularly at Waterloo obtained him twice the thanks of Parliament and eventually the barony and earldom of Stratford. And as it happens, their service in different spheres continues to this day.

What - finally - are we to make of all this?
You, officers of tomorrow, called to take up arms.

You, who must lead by example in a very different world.

First - salute, please, a victim of a very great injustice.
Admiral Byng was not the greatest naval tactician of his time – far from it. He was probably a rather cautious man, rigidly determined to maintain the line of battle.

But nor did he act without reason. Sadly and unjustly, as I believe, pragmatism and realism were not enough.

From the outset he was let down by others. Undermanned - under equipped – a mouse dispatched to rescue a lion.

Relieving Minorca was an impossible mission. But failure to attempt the impossible brought political and public condemnation.

But who really failed their country in those troubled times?

In his History of the British Army, Fortescue said the unfortunate Admiral was shot because Newcastle deserved to hang.

(Pause)

You, also, today must live with those who comment and decide from far off, but do not, for the most part, serve under fire.

Who may spin or sell that which they have not fully researched.

Who carry public responsibility, but not normally on the front line.

Respect them and obey them: you have no choice.

Pray only that their mistakes will not imperil your lives and the lives of those whom you have the privilege to command.

And should their failures take your lives, hope there will be room in a free country for an honest examination and a just Verdict.

For the bottom line is this -

Our politicians who make our laws and choose our enemies and then determine our steps - do not fight our battles.

That as I said at the beginning will be your duty and your responsibility.

There is none heavier on this earth.

I have no doubt at all that, in the rich traditions of the Senior Service - you also will also serve the Crown and your Country with distinction.

It was ever thus.

Because - before and after Nelson - that is what you do.

Thank you.

Final Music – Cue 10 Loud

THE END

PRODUCTION NOTE - for Cast of 6.

Lectern used by 2SL

On one Side -

3RD Voice

Byng

On the other Side -

First Voice

Fourth Voice

Witness Box

Second Voice

1. When the Opening Music [March] is being played, the Second Sea Lord, Byng and Voices 1, 3 and 4 enter and take their places. All march, save the 4th Voice. The Second Voice sits in the Witness Box.

131

2. At the Interval:

4th Voice exits first, followed by Voices 1, 2SL, Byng, 3 and 2 through Stage Left

3. **Curtain**: all bow taking cue from 2SL.

Nigel Pascoe

Lightning Source UK Ltd.
Milton Keynes UK
UKHW020723130319
339052UK00008B/139/P